Many instrume...
they cannot *vis*...
way a pianist c...

This little book will help you to form a *picture* of how the major scales are made up (tones, semitones, sharps and flats). Ask your teacher to explain.

The name of each scale is your starting note. After that all you need to remember is the alphabet!

Before you start to play the scale say the names of the notes starting at the bottom of the page thinking of the musical alphabet. Circles coloured in yellow mean add a sharp to the letter name and circles coloured in blue mean add a flat. (The letter names of the scales have not been written in so as to encourage you to remember the *musical* alphabet.)

After asking many pupils which colours they associated with sharps and flats, I found that most thought of sharps as bright colours (such as yellow and red) and flats as deeper colours (such as green and blue). I have chosen yellow and blue!

Use this little book to get to know the major scales; when you can play one octave extend the scale to two or more! Have fun!

C major

G major

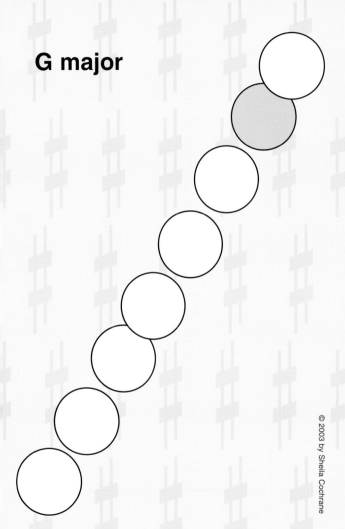

D major

A major

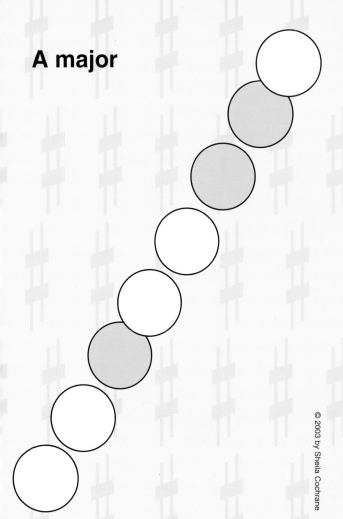

E major

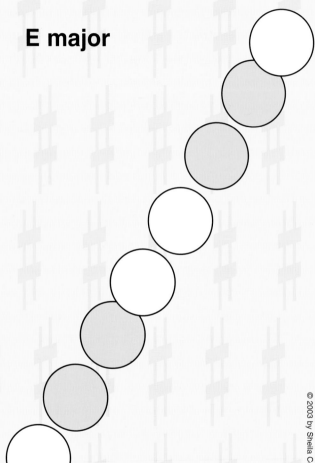

B major

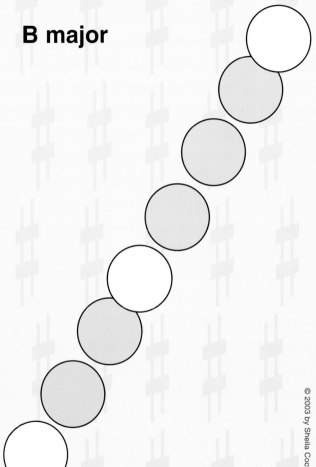

F♯ major

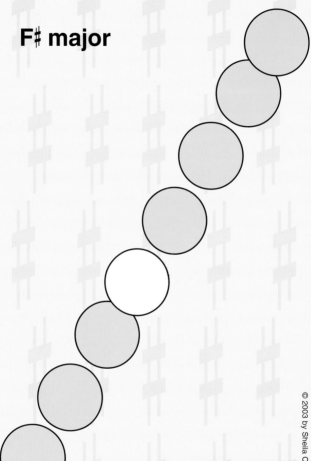

C# major

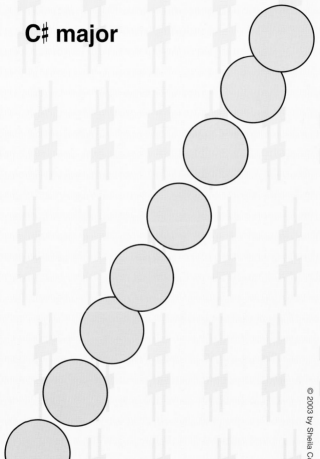

C major

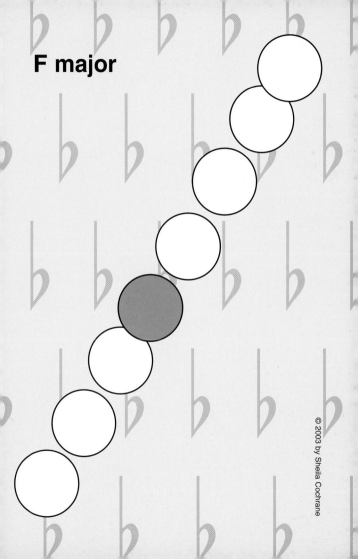

F major

B♭ major

E♭ major

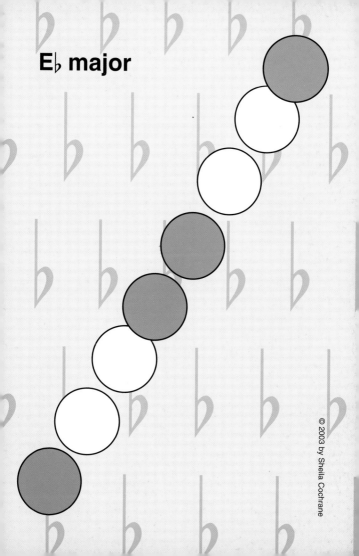

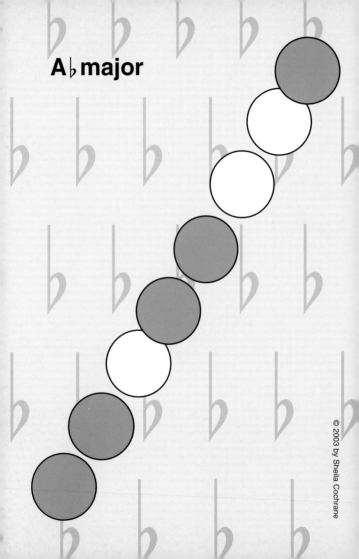

A♭ major

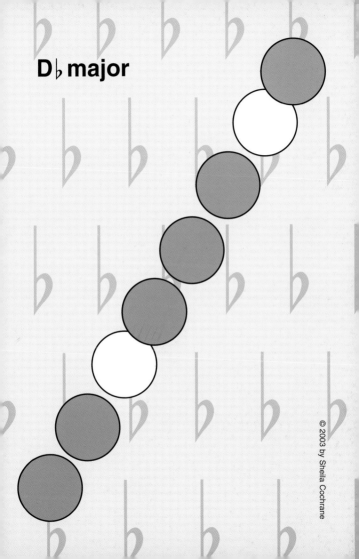

D♭ major

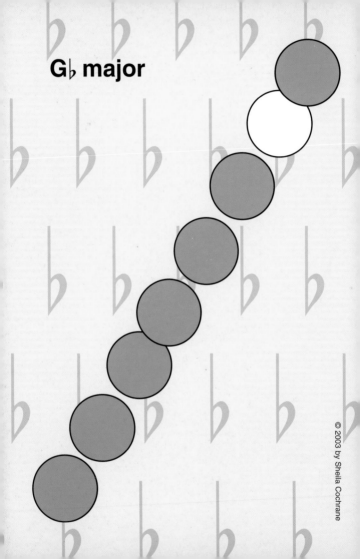

G♭ major

C♭ major

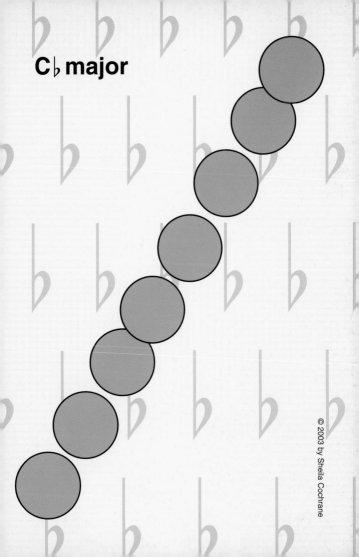

NOTES

NOTES

NOTES